50 Hot Chocolate Flavors from Around the World

By: Kelly Johnson

Table of Contents

- Classic Mexican Hot Chocolate
- Swiss Hot Chocolate with Whipped Cream
- Italian Cioccolata Calda
- French Hot Chocolate with Chantilly Cream
- Belgian Hot Chocolate with Speculoos
- Spanish Chocolate a la Taza
- Argentine Hot Chocolate with Dulce de Leche
- Turkish Hot Chocolate with Rosewater
- Jamaican Hot Chocolate with Cinnamon and Nutmeg
- American S'mores Hot Chocolate
- Brazilian Hot Chocolate with Condensed Milk
- Thai Hot Chocolate with Coconut Milk
- Indian Hot Chocolate with Cardamom
- Australian Hot Chocolate with Marshmallows
- Moroccan Hot Chocolate with Cinnamon and Orange
- Canadian Hot Chocolate with Maple Syrup
- Vietnamese Hot Chocolate with Coconut
- Filipino Tsokolate with Pili Nuts
- Chilean Hot Chocolate with Chile and Cinnamon
- British Hot Chocolate with Orange Zest
- Peruvian Hot Chocolate with Andean Spices
- Mexican Hot Chocolate with Chili and Vanilla
- Egyptian Hot Chocolate with Spices
- Puerto Rican Hot Chocolate with Rum
- Ecuadorian Hot Chocolate with Cinnamon
- South African Hot Chocolate with Rooibos
- Greek Hot Chocolate with Mastiha
- Irish Hot Chocolate with Whiskey
- Danish Hot Chocolate with Licorice
- Dutch Hot Chocolate with Stroopwafels
- Swedish Hot Chocolate with Lingonberries
- Finnish Hot Chocolate with Cloudberry Jam
- Colombian Hot Chocolate with Cheese
- Korean Hot Chocolate with Sweet Red Beans
- New Zealand Hot Chocolate with Hokey Pokey

- Lebanese Hot Chocolate with Orange Blossom
- Russian Hot Chocolate with Peppermint
- Polish Hot Chocolate with Honey and Lemon
- Malaysian Hot Chocolate with Pandan
- Indonesian Hot Chocolate with Palm Sugar
- Greek Hot Chocolate with Greek Yogurt
- Finnish Hot Chocolate with Mämmi
- Vietnamese Hot Chocolate with Pandan Leaves
- Croatian Hot Chocolate with Maraschino Liqueur
- Hungarian Hot Chocolate with Cinnamon Stick
- Icelandic Hot Chocolate with Blueberry Jam
- Kenyan Hot Chocolate with Spices
- Tanzanian Hot Chocolate with Ginger
- Nepalese Hot Chocolate with Tea Spices
- Bolivian Hot Chocolate with Cocoa Nibs

Classic Mexican Hot Chocolate

Ingredients:

- 2 cups whole milk
- 2 oz Mexican chocolate (Ibarra or Abuelita)
- 1 tbsp sugar (optional)
- 1 cinnamon stick
- 1/4 tsp vanilla extract
- Pinch of chili powder (optional)

Instructions:

1. In a small saucepan, heat the milk over medium heat.
2. Break the Mexican chocolate into pieces and add it to the milk, stirring until it dissolves completely.
3. Add the cinnamon stick and simmer for 2-3 minutes.
4. Stir in the vanilla extract and chili powder, if using.
5. Remove from heat and serve, garnished with a sprinkle of cinnamon or whipped cream, if desired.

Swiss Hot Chocolate with Whipped Cream

Ingredients:

- 2 cups whole milk
- 1/2 cup heavy cream
- 4 oz high-quality dark chocolate, chopped
- 1 tbsp sugar (optional)
- Whipped cream for topping

Instructions:

1. In a saucepan, combine the milk and heavy cream. Heat over medium heat until warm, but not boiling.
2. Remove from heat and whisk in the chopped dark chocolate until smooth.
3. Sweeten with sugar, if desired.
4. Pour into mugs and top with whipped cream before serving.

Italian Cioccolata Calda

Ingredients:

- 2 cups whole milk
- 3 oz dark chocolate, chopped
- 2 tbsp sugar
- 2 tbsp cornstarch
- Whipped cream for topping

Instructions:

1. In a small saucepan, whisk together the milk and cornstarch over medium heat.
2. Once the milk is warm, add the chopped dark chocolate and sugar, stirring continuously until smooth and thickened (about 5-7 minutes).
3. Pour into mugs and top with whipped cream. Serve hot.

French Hot Chocolate with Chantilly Cream

Ingredients:

- 2 cups whole milk
- 2 oz bittersweet chocolate, chopped
- 1 tbsp sugar
- 1/4 tsp vanilla extract
- 1/2 cup heavy cream
- 1 tbsp powdered sugar

Instructions:

1. In a saucepan, heat the milk over medium heat until warm.
2. Stir in the chopped chocolate and sugar, whisking until smooth and creamy.
3. Remove from heat and add vanilla extract.
4. In a separate bowl, whip the heavy cream with powdered sugar until soft peaks form.
5. Pour the hot chocolate into mugs and top with Chantilly cream.

Belgian Hot Chocolate with Speculoos

Ingredients:

- 2 cups whole milk
- 3 oz milk chocolate, chopped
- 2 speculoos cookies, crumbled
- 1 tbsp sugar (optional)
- Whipped cream for topping

Instructions:

1. In a saucepan, heat the milk over medium heat.
2. Add the chopped milk chocolate and stir until melted and smooth.
3. Add the crumbled speculoos cookies and sugar, if desired. Stir until combined.
4. Pour into mugs and top with whipped cream and additional cookie crumbles.

Spanish Chocolate a la Taza

Ingredients:

- 2 cups whole milk
- 3 oz bittersweet chocolate, chopped
- 1 cinnamon stick
- 1 tbsp sugar (optional)

Instructions:

1. Heat the milk and cinnamon stick in a saucepan over medium heat until warm.
2. Add the chopped bittersweet chocolate and stir until melted.
3. Sweeten with sugar, if desired.
4. Serve hot, with a sprinkle of cinnamon or whipped cream.

Argentine Hot Chocolate with Dulce de Leche

Ingredients:

- 2 cups whole milk
- 2 oz dark chocolate, chopped
- 2 tbsp dulce de leche
- 1/4 tsp vanilla extract

Instructions:

1. Heat the milk over medium heat in a saucepan.
2. Add the chopped dark chocolate and dulce de leche, stirring until completely melted and smooth.
3. Stir in the vanilla extract.
4. Pour into mugs and serve hot.

Turkish Hot Chocolate with Rosewater

Ingredients:

- 2 cups whole milk
- 3 oz dark chocolate, chopped
- 1 tbsp sugar (optional)
- 1/2 tsp rosewater
- Whipped cream for topping

Instructions:

1. In a saucepan, heat the milk over medium heat.
2. Add the chopped dark chocolate and sugar, stirring until smooth.
3. Remove from heat and stir in the rosewater.
4. Pour into mugs and top with whipped cream.

Jamaican Hot Chocolate with Cinnamon and Nutmeg

Ingredients:

- 2 cups whole milk
- 2 oz dark chocolate, chopped
- 1 tsp ground cinnamon
- 1/2 tsp ground nutmeg
- 1 tbsp sugar (optional)
- A pinch of salt

Instructions:

1. In a saucepan, heat the milk over medium heat until warm.
2. Add the chopped dark chocolate and stir until melted.
3. Stir in the cinnamon, nutmeg, and sugar, if using.
4. Simmer for a few more minutes, then remove from heat.
5. Pour into mugs and serve hot with a sprinkle of cinnamon or whipped cream.

American S'mores Hot Chocolate

Ingredients:

- 2 cups whole milk
- 2 oz milk chocolate, chopped
- 1 tbsp sugar
- 1/4 tsp vanilla extract
- 2 tbsp graham cracker crumbs
- 1 large marshmallow, toasted

Instructions:

1. Heat the milk in a saucepan over medium heat until warm.
2. Stir in the milk chocolate and sugar until smooth.
3. Add the vanilla extract and continue to stir.
4. Pour into mugs, top with graham cracker crumbs and a toasted marshmallow for a classic s'mores flavor.

Brazilian Hot Chocolate with Condensed Milk

Ingredients:

- 2 cups whole milk
- 3 oz dark chocolate, chopped
- 2 tbsp sweetened condensed milk
- 1 tbsp sugar (optional)

Instructions:

1. In a saucepan, combine the milk and dark chocolate.
2. Heat over medium heat, stirring constantly until the chocolate is melted.
3. Stir in the sweetened condensed milk and sugar, if desired, until smooth and creamy.
4. Pour into mugs and serve hot.

Thai Hot Chocolate with Coconut Milk

Ingredients:

- 2 cups coconut milk
- 2 oz dark chocolate, chopped
- 1 tbsp sugar (optional)
- 1/4 tsp vanilla extract
- A pinch of sea salt

Instructions:

1. Heat the coconut milk in a saucepan over medium heat.
2. Add the chopped dark chocolate and stir until fully melted and smooth.
3. Stir in sugar and vanilla extract, adjusting sweetness as desired.
4. Pour into mugs, sprinkle with sea salt, and serve hot.

Indian Hot Chocolate with Cardamom

Ingredients:

- 2 cups whole milk
- 2 oz dark chocolate, chopped
- 1/2 tsp ground cardamom
- 1 tbsp sugar (optional)
- A pinch of ground cinnamon

Instructions:

1. Heat the milk in a saucepan over medium heat.
2. Add the chopped dark chocolate and stir until melted.
3. Stir in cardamom, cinnamon, and sugar, if desired.
4. Simmer for a few minutes, then remove from heat.
5. Pour into mugs and serve hot.

Australian Hot Chocolate with Marshmallows

Ingredients:

- 2 cups whole milk
- 2 oz milk chocolate, chopped
- 1 tbsp sugar
- 1/4 tsp vanilla extract
- 2-3 marshmallows, toasted

Instructions:

1. In a saucepan, heat the milk over medium heat until warm.
2. Stir in the milk chocolate and sugar until melted and smooth.
3. Add the vanilla extract and mix.
4. Pour into mugs and top with toasted marshmallows.

Moroccan Hot Chocolate with Cinnamon and Orange

Ingredients:

- 2 cups whole milk
- 2 oz dark chocolate, chopped
- 1/4 tsp ground cinnamon
- Zest of 1 orange
- 1 tbsp sugar (optional)

Instructions:

1. Heat the milk over medium heat in a saucepan.
2. Add the chopped dark chocolate and stir until fully melted.
3. Stir in the cinnamon, orange zest, and sugar, if desired.
4. Simmer for a few more minutes, then remove from heat.
5. Pour into mugs and serve hot.

Canadian Hot Chocolate with Maple Syrup

Ingredients:

- 2 cups whole milk
- 2 oz dark chocolate, chopped
- 1 tbsp maple syrup
- 1/4 tsp vanilla extract

Instructions:

1. Heat the milk in a saucepan over medium heat until warm.
2. Add the chopped dark chocolate and stir until melted and smooth.
3. Stir in the maple syrup and vanilla extract.
4. Pour into mugs and serve hot.

Vietnamese Hot Chocolate with Coconut

Ingredients:

- 2 cups coconut milk
- 2 oz dark chocolate, chopped
- 1 tbsp sugar (optional)
- 1/4 tsp vanilla extract
- 1 tbsp shredded coconut (for garnish)

Instructions:

1. Heat the coconut milk in a saucepan over medium heat.
2. Stir in the chopped dark chocolate and sugar until melted and smooth.
3. Add the vanilla extract and mix.
4. Pour into mugs and garnish with shredded coconut. Serve hot.

Filipino Tsokolate with Pili Nuts

Ingredients:

- 2 cups whole milk
- 2 oz Filipino tablea chocolate (or dark chocolate)
- 1 tbsp sugar (optional)
- 1/4 tsp vanilla extract
- 2 tbsp crushed pili nuts (for garnish)
Instructions:
1. Heat the milk in a saucepan over medium heat.
2. Add the tablea chocolate and stir until it melts.
3. Stir in the sugar and vanilla extract until smooth.
4. Pour into mugs and garnish with crushed pili nuts.

Chilean Hot Chocolate with Chile and Cinnamon

Ingredients:

- 2 cups whole milk
- 2 oz dark chocolate, chopped
- 1/2 tsp ground cinnamon
- 1/4 tsp ground chili powder (or cayenne)
- 1 tbsp sugar (optional)

Instructions:

1. Heat the milk over medium heat in a saucepan.
2. Add the chopped dark chocolate and stir until melted and smooth.
3. Stir in the cinnamon, chili powder, and sugar, if desired.
4. Simmer for a few minutes, then pour into mugs and serve hot.

British Hot Chocolate with Orange Zest

Ingredients:

- 2 cups whole milk
- 2 oz milk chocolate, chopped
- Zest of 1 orange
- 1 tbsp sugar (optional)
- 1/4 tsp vanilla extract

Instructions:

1. Heat the milk over medium heat until warm.
2. Stir in the chopped milk chocolate until melted and smooth.
3. Add the orange zest, sugar, and vanilla extract.
4. Stir to combine, then pour into mugs and serve hot.

Peruvian Hot Chocolate with Andean Spices

Ingredients:

- 2 cups whole milk
- 2 oz dark chocolate, chopped
- 1/4 tsp ground cinnamon
- 1/4 tsp ground cloves
- 1/4 tsp ground nutmeg
- 1 tbsp sugar (optional)

Instructions:

1. Heat the milk in a saucepan over medium heat.
2. Add the chopped dark chocolate and stir until melted.
3. Stir in the cinnamon, cloves, nutmeg, and sugar, if desired.
4. Simmer for a few minutes, then pour into mugs and serve hot.

Mexican Hot Chocolate with Chili and Vanilla

Ingredients:

- 2 cups whole milk
- 2 oz dark chocolate, chopped
- 1/2 tsp ground cinnamon
- 1/4 tsp chili powder or cayenne pepper
- 1/2 tsp vanilla extract
- 1 tbsp sugar (optional)

Instructions:

1. Heat the milk over medium heat in a saucepan.
2. Stir in the chopped dark chocolate until fully melted.
3. Add the cinnamon, chili powder, vanilla extract, and sugar, if desired.
4. Stir until smooth, then pour into mugs and serve hot.

Egyptian Hot Chocolate with Spices

Ingredients:

- 2 cups whole milk
- 2 oz dark chocolate, chopped
- 1/4 tsp ground cinnamon
- 1/4 tsp ground cardamom
- 1 tbsp sugar (optional)
- A pinch of ground cloves

Instructions:

1. Heat the milk in a saucepan over medium heat.
2. Add the chopped dark chocolate and stir until melted.
3. Stir in the cinnamon, cardamom, cloves, and sugar, if using.
4. Simmer for a few minutes, then remove from heat and pour into mugs. Serve hot.

Puerto Rican Hot Chocolate with Rum

Ingredients:

- 2 cups whole milk
- 2 oz dark chocolate, chopped
- 1 tbsp sugar (optional)
- 1/4 tsp ground cinnamon
- 1 tbsp dark rum

Instructions:

1. Heat the milk in a saucepan over medium heat until warm.
2. Stir in the chopped dark chocolate and sugar until smooth.
3. Add the cinnamon and rum, then stir to combine.
4. Simmer for a few minutes, then pour into mugs and serve hot.

Ecuadorian Hot Chocolate with Cinnamon

Ingredients:

- 2 cups whole milk
- 2 oz Ecuadorian dark chocolate, chopped
- 1/2 tsp ground cinnamon
- 1 tbsp sugar (optional)

Instructions:

1. Heat the milk over medium heat in a saucepan.
2. Stir in the chopped Ecuadorian dark chocolate and cinnamon, letting it melt and blend together.
3. Add sugar, if desired, and stir until smooth.
4. Pour into mugs and serve hot.

South African Hot Chocolate with Rooibos

Ingredients:

- 2 cups whole milk
- 2 oz dark chocolate, chopped
- 1 tbsp rooibos tea leaves (or 1 rooibos tea bag)
- 1 tbsp sugar (optional)

Instructions:

1. Heat the milk in a saucepan over medium heat until warm.
2. Add the rooibos tea and simmer for about 5 minutes.
3. Remove the tea leaves or tea bag, then stir in the chopped dark chocolate and sugar until melted and smooth.
4. Pour into mugs and serve hot.

Greek Hot Chocolate with Mastiha

Ingredients:

- 2 cups whole milk
- 2 oz dark chocolate, chopped
- 1/4 tsp mastiha (Greek resin)
- 1 tbsp sugar (optional)

Instructions:

1. Heat the milk in a saucepan over medium heat.
2. Stir in the chopped dark chocolate and mastiha, letting the chocolate melt completely.
3. Add sugar if desired, and stir until smooth.
4. Pour into mugs and serve hot.

Irish Hot Chocolate with Whiskey

Ingredients:

- 2 cups whole milk
- 2 oz dark chocolate, chopped
- 1 tbsp sugar (optional)
- 1 oz Irish whiskey
- 1/4 tsp vanilla extract

Instructions:

1. Heat the milk over medium heat until warm.
2. Stir in the chopped dark chocolate until fully melted.
3. Add sugar and vanilla extract, and stir to combine.
4. Remove from heat and stir in the Irish whiskey.
5. Pour into mugs and serve hot.

Danish Hot Chocolate with Licorice

Ingredients:

- 2 cups whole milk
- 2 oz dark chocolate, chopped
- 1/2 tsp ground licorice powder (or 1 licorice candy, melted)
- 1 tbsp sugar (optional)

Instructions:

1. Heat the milk in a saucepan over medium heat.
2. Add the chopped dark chocolate and licorice powder (or melted licorice candy). Stir until smooth.
3. Add sugar if desired, and stir until fully combined.
4. Pour into mugs and serve hot.

Dutch Hot Chocolate with Stroopwafels

Ingredients:

- 2 cups whole milk
- 2 oz dark chocolate, chopped
- 1 tbsp sugar (optional)
- 1 stroopwafel (Dutch caramel waffle)
  Instructions:
1. Heat the milk over medium heat in a saucepan until warm.
2. Stir in the chopped dark chocolate and sugar until melted and smooth.
3. Pour into mugs and top with a stroopwafel, allowing it to soften and slightly melt into the hot chocolate.
4. Serve hot.

Swedish Hot Chocolate with Lingonberries

Ingredients:

- 2 cups whole milk
- 2 oz dark chocolate, chopped
- 1/4 cup lingonberry jam or fresh lingonberries
- 1 tbsp sugar (optional)

Instructions:

1. Heat the milk in a saucepan over medium heat.
2. Stir in the chopped dark chocolate until fully melted.
3. Add the lingonberry jam or fresh lingonberries, and sugar if desired.
4. Stir to combine and pour into mugs.
5. Serve hot, garnished with a few lingonberries if desired.

Finnish Hot Chocolate with Cloudberry Jam

Ingredients:

- 2 cups whole milk
- 2 oz dark chocolate, chopped
- 1 tbsp cloudberry jam
- 1 tbsp sugar (optional)

Instructions:

1. Heat the milk in a saucepan over medium heat.
2. Stir in the chopped dark chocolate until melted and smooth.
3. Add the cloudberry jam and sugar if desired, and stir until well combined.
4. Pour into mugs and serve hot.

Colombian Hot Chocolate with Cheese
Ingredients:

- 2 cups whole milk
- 2 oz Colombian chocolate (or bittersweet chocolate), chopped
- 1 tbsp sugar (optional)
- 1/4 cup shredded cheese (like queso fresco or mozzarella)

Instructions:

1. Heat the milk in a saucepan over medium heat until warm.
2. Stir in the chopped Colombian chocolate and sugar until the chocolate is fully melted.
3. Pour into a mug, then top with shredded cheese.
4. Serve hot, allowing the cheese to melt into the chocolate.

Korean Hot Chocolate with Sweet Red Beans
Ingredients:

- 2 cups whole milk
- 2 oz dark chocolate, chopped
- 1/4 cup sweet red bean paste (anko)
- 1 tbsp sugar (optional)
  Instructions:
1. Heat the milk over medium heat in a saucepan until warm.
2. Stir in the chopped dark chocolate until it melts and combines.
3. Add sweet red bean paste and sugar, stirring until smooth.
4. Pour into mugs and serve hot with a spoonful of the sweet red bean paste at the bottom.

New Zealand Hot Chocolate with Hokey Pokey
Ingredients:

- 2 cups whole milk
- 2 oz dark chocolate, chopped
- 1/4 cup Hokey Pokey toffee (or honeycomb candy), chopped into small pieces
- 1 tbsp sugar (optional)

Instructions:
1. Heat the milk over medium heat in a saucepan until warm.
2. Stir in the chopped dark chocolate until it's fully melted and smooth.
3. Add sugar if desired, and stir until combined.
4. Pour into mugs and top with chopped Hokey Pokey pieces.
5. Serve hot with a crunchy toffee topping.

Lebanese Hot Chocolate with Orange Blossom
Ingredients:

- 2 cups whole milk
- 2 oz dark chocolate, chopped
- 1/2 tsp orange blossom water
- 1 tbsp sugar (optional)
  Instructions:
1. Heat the milk over medium heat until warm.
2. Stir in the chopped dark chocolate until fully melted and smooth.
3. Add orange blossom water and sugar if desired, stirring well.
4. Pour into mugs and serve hot, allowing the fragrant orange blossom scent to infuse the chocolate.

Russian Hot Chocolate with Peppermint
Ingredients:

- 2 cups whole milk
- 2 oz dark chocolate, chopped
- 1/4 tsp peppermint extract
- 1 tbsp sugar (optional)

Instructions:

1. Heat the milk in a saucepan over medium heat until warm.
2. Stir in the chopped dark chocolate until melted and smooth.
3. Add peppermint extract and sugar, and stir well.
4. Pour into mugs and serve hot, optionally garnished with peppermint leaves.

Polish Hot Chocolate with Honey and Lemon
Ingredients:

- 2 cups whole milk
- 2 oz dark chocolate, chopped
- 1 tbsp honey
- 1 tsp fresh lemon juice

Instructions:
1. Heat the milk over medium heat until warm.
2. Stir in the chopped dark chocolate until it's fully melted and smooth.
3. Add honey and lemon juice, and stir to combine.
4. Pour into mugs and serve hot, with a lemon twist if desired.

Malaysian Hot Chocolate with Pandan

Ingredients:

- 2 cups whole milk
- 2 oz dark chocolate, chopped
- 1 tbsp pandan paste or pandan leaves (for infusion)
- 1 tbsp sugar (optional)

Instructions:

1. Heat the milk over medium heat with pandan paste or pandan leaves (if using leaves, remove them before serving).
2. Stir in the chopped dark chocolate until it's fully melted and smooth.
3. Add sugar if desired, and stir until combined.
4. Pour into mugs and serve hot with a light pandan aroma.

Indonesian Hot Chocolate with Palm Sugar
Ingredients:

- 2 cups whole milk
- 2 oz dark chocolate, chopped
- 1 tbsp palm sugar, grated
- 1/4 tsp cinnamon (optional)

Instructions:

1. Heat the milk in a saucepan over medium heat until warm.
2. Stir in the chopped dark chocolate until melted and smooth.
3. Add the grated palm sugar and cinnamon, stirring until fully dissolved.
4. Pour into mugs and serve hot with a rich, caramel-like sweetness.

Greek Hot Chocolate with Greek Yogurt

Ingredients:

- 2 cups whole milk
- 2 oz dark chocolate, chopped
- 1/4 cup Greek yogurt
- 1 tbsp honey (optional)

Instructions:

1. Heat the milk in a saucepan over medium heat until warm.
2. Stir in the chopped dark chocolate until fully melted and smooth.
3. Remove from heat and whisk in Greek yogurt and honey until well combined.
4. Pour into mugs and serve hot, with a dollop of extra yogurt on top if desired.

Finnish Hot Chocolate with Mämmi
Ingredients:

- 2 cups whole milk
- 2 oz dark chocolate, chopped
- 1/4 cup mämmi (Finnish malted rye pudding)
- 1 tbsp sugar (optional)

Instructions:
1. Heat the milk in a saucepan over medium heat until warm.
2. Stir in the chopped dark chocolate until fully melted.
3. Add mämmi and sugar, mixing well to create a smooth and creamy texture.
4. Pour into mugs and serve hot, with a little extra mämmi as garnish if desired.

Vietnamese Hot Chocolate with Pandan Leaves
Ingredients:

- 2 cups whole milk
- 2 oz dark chocolate, chopped
- 1 pandan leaf (or 1 tsp pandan paste)
- 1 tbsp sugar (optional)

Instructions:

1. Heat the milk with the pandan leaf in a saucepan over medium heat. If using pandan paste, stir it in after the milk is warmed.
2. Once the milk is fragrant with pandan, remove the leaf (if used) and stir in the chopped dark chocolate until melted.
3. Add sugar if desired and stir until fully combined.
4. Pour into mugs and serve hot with a lingering pandan aroma.

Croatian Hot Chocolate with Maraschino Liqueur

Ingredients:

- 2 cups whole milk
- 2 oz dark chocolate, chopped
- 1 tbsp maraschino liqueur
- 1 tbsp sugar (optional)

Instructions:

1. Heat the milk over medium heat until warm.
2. Stir in the chopped dark chocolate until fully melted and smooth.
3. Add the maraschino liqueur and sugar, and mix well.
4. Pour into mugs and serve hot, with a cherry garnish if desired.

Hungarian Hot Chocolate with Cinnamon Stick
Ingredients:

- 2 cups whole milk
- 2 oz dark chocolate, chopped
- 1 cinnamon stick
- 1 tbsp sugar (optional)

Instructions:
1. Heat the milk with the cinnamon stick over medium heat until warm, allowing the cinnamon to infuse the milk.
2. Stir in the chopped dark chocolate until fully melted and smooth.
3. Add sugar if desired, and stir well.
4. Remove the cinnamon stick and pour the hot chocolate into mugs. Serve hot with a dash of extra cinnamon on top.

Icelandic Hot Chocolate with Blueberry Jam
Ingredients:

- 2 cups whole milk
- 2 oz dark chocolate, chopped
- 2 tbsp blueberry jam
- 1 tbsp sugar (optional)

Instructions:

1. Heat the milk in a saucepan over medium heat until warm.
2. Stir in the chopped dark chocolate until fully melted and smooth.
3. Add the blueberry jam and sugar (if desired), whisking until combined and smooth.
4. Pour into mugs and serve hot, garnished with a spoonful of blueberry jam if desired.

Kenyan Hot Chocolate with Spices

Ingredients:

- 2 cups whole milk
- 2 oz dark chocolate, chopped
- 1/4 tsp ground ginger
- 1/4 tsp ground cinnamon
- Pinch of ground cloves
- 1 tbsp sugar (optional)

Instructions:

1. Heat the milk in a saucepan over medium heat.
2. Stir in the chopped dark chocolate and spices until fully melted and smooth.
3. Add sugar if desired and stir well.
4. Pour into mugs and serve hot, with a pinch of cinnamon or ginger on top for extra flavor.

Tanzanian Hot Chocolate with Ginger
Ingredients:

- 2 cups whole milk
- 2 oz dark chocolate, chopped
- 1 tbsp fresh ginger, grated
- 1 tbsp sugar (optional)

Instructions:

1. Heat the milk in a saucepan over medium heat, adding the grated ginger to infuse flavor.
2. Once the milk is warm, remove the ginger and stir in the chopped dark chocolate until melted and smooth.
3. Add sugar if desired and mix well.
4. Pour into mugs and serve hot, with an extra slice of ginger for garnish if desired.

Nepalese Hot Chocolate with Tea Spices
Ingredients:

- 2 cups whole milk
- 2 oz dark chocolate, chopped
- 1/4 tsp ground cardamom
- 1/4 tsp ground cinnamon
- 1/4 tsp ground cloves
- 1 tbsp sugar (optional)

Instructions:

1. Heat the milk with the spices over medium heat, allowing them to infuse the milk with flavor.
2. Stir in the chopped dark chocolate until fully melted and smooth.
3. Add sugar if desired and stir until combined.
4. Pour into mugs and serve hot, garnished with a dash of extra cinnamon or cardamom.

Bolivian Hot Chocolate with Cocoa Nibs
Ingredients:

- 2 cups whole milk
- 2 oz dark chocolate, chopped
- 1 tbsp cocoa nibs
- 1 tbsp sugar (optional)

Instructions:

1. Heat the milk in a saucepan over medium heat until warm.
2. Stir in the chopped dark chocolate until fully melted and smooth.
3. Add the cocoa nibs and sugar (if desired), mixing well.
4. Pour into mugs and serve hot, topped with extra cocoa nibs for crunch.